Contents

Being honest means telling
the truth.

Being honest means people can trust you.

When you return something that
is not yours ...

you are being honest.

When you own up to making a
mess ...

you are being honest.

When you tell someone you made
a mistake ...

you are being honest.

When you say,
"I've had my share" ...

you are being honest.

When you say,
"I've had my turn" …

you are being honest.

When you tell someone how
you feel ...

you are being honest.

When you admit that you
were wrong ...

you are being honest.

Being honest is important.

How can you be honest?

Activity

How is this boy being honest?

Picture glossary

 **admit** tell something that you may be afraid to tell

 **honest** always telling the truth

 **trust** to believe in someone

Index

Note to Parents and Teachers

Before reading
Talk to the children about being honest. Why is it important to be honest? Is it always easy to be honest? Why not?

After reading
• Create a role play demonstrating honesty and dishonesty. For example, drop a coin from your purse. Challenge the children: What is the honest thing for someone to do? Encourage a child to do the honest thing and then praise them for their honesty. Make other little role plays around owning up and saying sorry.
• Talk to the children about saying sorry. Ask when they should say sorry and how they feel when they have to say sorry. Give each child a paper plate. Tell them to draw their own faces on the plate. They may like to give themselves hair made of wool to stick on the top of the plate. Encourage them to think about the expression on their faces. Are they happy, or sad?
• Say a rhyme with the children to help them say sorry to each other or to adults. For example: I'm sorry if I hurt you, or said something unkind. I'm sorry if you feel upset, Next time I'll be more kind.